CIVICS
Q & A

HOW DO LAWS GET PASSED?

Leslie Harper

PowerKiDS press™

New York

Published in 2013 by The Rosen Publishing Group, Inc.
29 East 21st Street, New York, NY 10010

First Edition

Editor: Jennifer Way
Book Design: Ashley Drago
Layout Design: Andrew Povolny

Photo Credits: Cover, p. 20 Chris Grill/Getty Images; p. 4 UniversalImageGroup/Getty Images; p. 5 (top & bottom) Auremar/Shutterstock.com; p. 6 Rick Scibelli/Getty Images; p. 7 Jamal Countless/Getty Images; p. 9 Cristina Ciochina/Shutterstock.com; p. 10 Boston Globe/Getty Images; pp. 11, 13 Scott J. Ferrell/CQ-Roll Call Group/Getty Images; p. 12 Tom Williams/CQ-Roll Call Group/Getty Images; p. 15 Jim Watson/AFP/Getty Images; p. 16 Saul Loeb/AFP/Getty Images; p. 17 (top) AFP/Getty Images; p. 17 (bottom) Diana Walker/Time & Life Images/Getty Images; p. 18 David McNew/Getty Images; p. 19 //commons.wikimedia.org/File:US_initiatives,_referenda_map.jpg; p. 21 Jupiterimages/Creatas/Thinkstock.

Library of Congress Cataloging-in-Publication Data

Harper, Leslie.
 How do laws get passed? / by Leslie Harper. — 1st ed.
    p. cm. — (Civics Q&A)
 Includes index.
 ISBN 978-1-4488-7436-1 (library binding) — ISBN 978-1-4488-7509-2 (pbk.) —
 ISBN 978-1-4488-7583-2 (6-pack)
 1. Legislation—United States—Juvenile literature. I. Title.
 KF4945.H37 2013
 328.73'077—dc23

                              2012001074

Manufactured in the United States of America

CPSIA Compliance Information: Batch #SW12PK: For Further Information contact Rosen Publishing, New York, New York at 1-800-237-9932

CONTENTS

For as long as people have lived together, there have been laws. Most laws are created to keep people safe. The earliest written laws that we know of are over 3,700 years old!

In the United States, we have many laws. There are laws that say how old you must be

The Code of Hammurabi is carved into this stone. Hammurabi was a king in ancient Babylon, over 3,700 years ago. His code was one of the first recorded bodies of laws.

4

before you can vote or drive a car. Laws tell us how fast we can drive on a road and when to stop. Laws tell us that we cannot hurt others or steal. When people obey laws, it makes it easier for everyone in a community to get along!

Hunting laws keep hunters safe and also control and protect animal populations.

Laws that control how houses are built keep us safe in our homes, and they keep the workers who build them safe, too.

Some laws, such as speed limits, differ from state to state. Texas has some of the highest speed limits in the United States.

Some laws apply only to a small area, such as a city or a county. Local governments make these laws. Local laws usually concern matters such as where you can park a car or how late at night you can make loud noises.

State laws apply to an entire state. The group that makes these laws is called the **state legislature**. Members of the legislature listen to the people of their state, then pass laws based on what those people want. That is why something may be legal in one state, but illegal, or against the law, in another state.

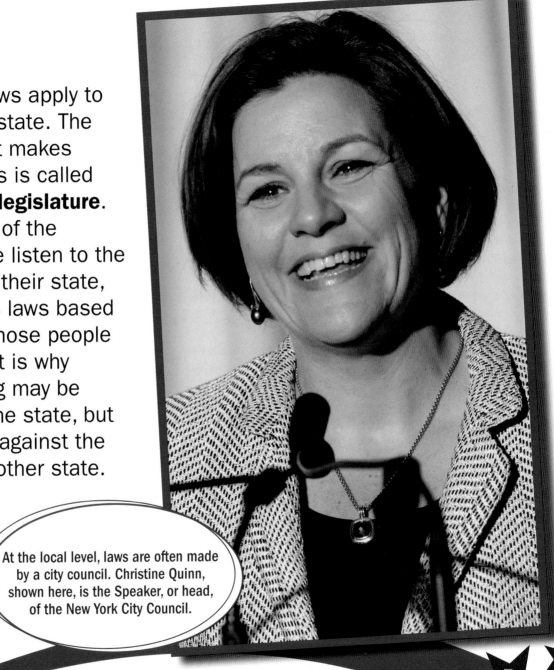

At the local level, laws are often made by a city council. Christine Quinn, shown here, is the Speaker, or head, of the New York City Council.

WHO MAKES FEDERAL LAWS?

In the United States, the **federal** government is divided into three branches. The branch that makes laws is called the **legislative** branch. It is made up of a group called **Congress**.

The US Congress is divided into two parts, called houses. The upper house is the Senate. Its members are senators. There are two senators from each state. The lower house is the House of Representatives. States have different numbers of representatives. States with higher populations have more representatives.

Congress passes many laws every year. These federal laws apply to everyone in the United States.

The Capitol, shown here, is where Congress meets to make laws. It is in Washington, D.C.

WHAT IS A BILL?

Massachusetts lawmakers applaud Governor Deval Patrick as he signs a bill into law. Representative Joseph Wagner (back, center) was the lead sponsor of the bill.

Laws begin as bills. A bill is a written suggestion for a law. Members of the federal legislature write federal bills, while state bills are written by state legislatures. The person who writes or introduces a bill is called its **sponsor**. Other members of the legislature who agree with the bill can also be listed as cosponsors.

A bill may be written in either house, and it will go through many of the same steps. First it will be given a number and read to the entire house. Then it will be sent to a **committee** to be read and studied.

Here, members of the House Committee on Ways and Means meet in 2005. This committee is important because all federal tax bills must pass through it.

Committees in the House of Representatives and the Senate are made up of experts, or people who know a lot about certain subjects. There are different committees for bills that deal with money, education, the environment, and many other things.

Members of the Senate Judiciary Committee, shown here, meet about people the president has picked to become federal judges before the Senate votes on whether to approve them.

When a bill goes to a committee, the members of that committee will read it carefully. They will research the reasons why it should or should not become a law. They can also make changes to the bill. If the members of the committee agree with a bill, they will send it back to the whole House or Senate for a vote.

Senator Daniel Inouye (front, left), of Hawaii, is head of one of the Senate's most powerful committees. It deals with government spending.

Before a vote is taken, members debate, or discuss, the bill. More changes can also be made to the bill. Then it is time for the vote. If the **majority** of the members vote that the bill should be a law, the bill has passed in that house.

Bills passed in one house are then sent to the other house for another vote. If a bill passes both houses, the vice president and the Speaker of the House, who leads the House of Representatives, sign it. Now the bill is ready to be sent to the president.

One of the duties of the vice president is to be president of the Senate. Here you can see Vice President Joseph Biden (left) and John Boehner (right), the Speaker of the House of Representatives.

When a bill is sent to the president, he can sign it and it becomes a law. He may also **veto**, or refuse to sign it. The president has 10 days to decide what to do. If he has not signed the bill after 10 days, it will become a law if Congress is still meeting. If Congress has finished meeting for the year, the bill will not become a law.

President Barack Obama is shown here signing the Lilly Ledbetter Fair Pay Act into law. This law makes it easier for female workers to fight for equal pay.

If the president vetoes a bill, Congress can decide to take another vote. If two-thirds of both houses vote for the bill, it becomes a law.

Here President John F. Kennedy signs a bill to speed up the space program's progress toward a Moon mission.

President Ronald Reagan receives applause after signing a tax reform bill into law.

The Californians shown here hold signs for and against certain propositions, or suggested laws. Proposition 74 was an initiative that failed to pass.

In some states, laws can be voted on directly by the people. When a person or group wants a new law, they can ask people who agree with them to sign a **petition**. If enough people sign it, an **initiative** can be put on the ballot during an election. Then the people of the state vote on it.

If someone does not like a law passed by the state legislature, he can also try to get enough people to sign a petition. A **referendum** on the ballot asks people if they would like to keep, change, or throw out a law that already exists.

States with Initiatives and Referendums

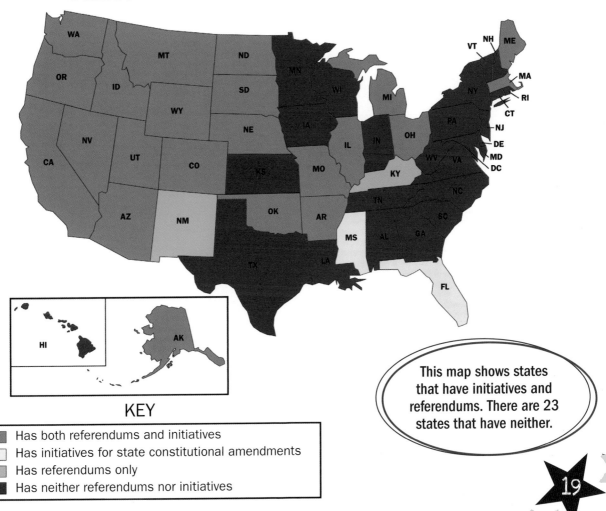

KEY

- Has both referendums and initiatives
- Has initiatives for state constitutional amendments
- Has referendums only
- Has neither referendums nor initiatives

This map shows states that have initiatives and referendums. There are 23 states that have neither.

19

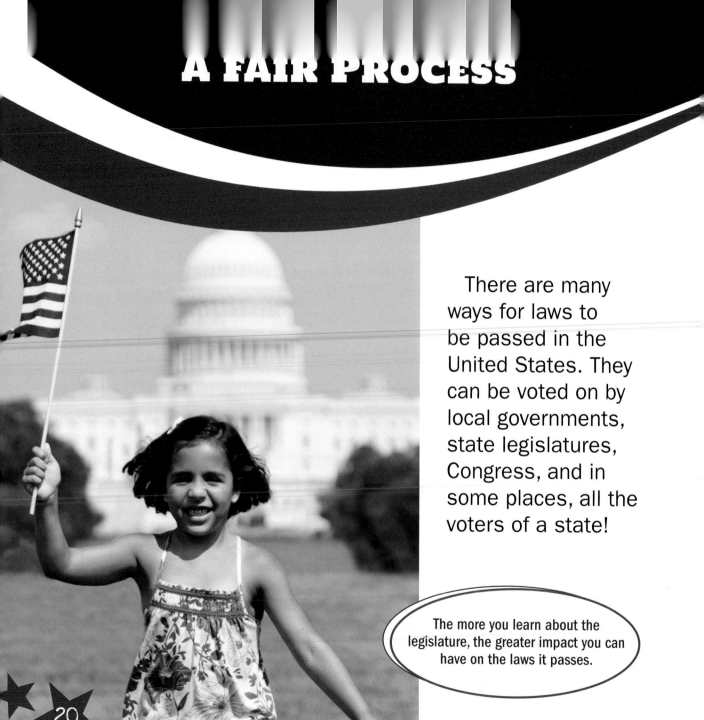

A FAIR PROCESS

There are many ways for laws to be passed in the United States. They can be voted on by local governments, state legislatures, Congress, and in some places, all the voters of a state!

The more you learn about the legislature, the greater impact you can have on the laws it passes.

Laws are one of the most important parts of our society. The way that they are created is important, too. By having debates and taking votes, we keep the process as fair as possible. New laws can be created, and old laws can be changed or thrown out. As peoples' ideas and beliefs change over time, laws can change with them!

One of the most powerful tools you will have to shape how laws are made is your vote. You will be able to vote for the people you want to make the laws!

LAWS Q&A

1

Q: Besides the legislative branch, what are the other two branches of government called?

A: **The other two branches are the executive branch and the judicial branch.**

2

Q: What is an amendment?

A: **An amendment is an addition or change to the US Constitution.**

3

Q: How many bills are introduced in Congress every year?

A: **Around 10,000 bills are introduced in Congress each year. Only a few hundred will become new laws, though.**

4

Q: What is a joint committee?

A: **A joint committee is made up of members of both the House of Representatives and the Senate. It is formed if one house would like to make important changes to a bill passed in the other house.**

5

Q: To what branch of government does the president belong?

A: **The president is the head of the executive branch. Having the president sign and approve laws is an example of checks and balances.**

6

Q: How many people are there in the House of Representatives and how many in the Senate?

A: **There are 435 members of the House of Representatives and 100 members of the Senate.**